The
Choral Ne Plus Ultras

Opus 10

Michael Bobb

<u>WORDS</u>

The Autograph Score is a **Michael Bobb Productions** imprint

Paperback
ISBN 9781738410668
1. Edition, 2025

www.michaelbobb.com
michaelbobbproductions@outlook.com

© Michael Bobb

All rights reserved

The rights of the published composer to be identified as the author of this work have been asserted in accordance with the
Copyright, Designs and Patents Act 1988

· London ·

Contents

1.	**ALMIGHTY GOD SAID…** Opus 10 No. 1	9
2.	**He is the Image of the Invisible God** Opus 10 No. 2	11
3.	**The Separating Veil is Torn!** Opus 10 No. 3	14
4.	**Christ the Rising Star** Blink to the Moon! Opus 10 No. 4	17
5.	**The Shulammite Woman** Opus 10 No. 5	20
6.	**My Eternal Peace** Opus 10 No. 6	22
7.	**The Alternative Three Magi!** Opus 10 No. 7	24
8.	**Jauchzet Frohlocket – After J. S. Bach** Opus 10 No. 8	26
9.	**The Seven Spirits of Christ** Opus 10 No. 9	28
10.	**Christ Jesus the Beau** Opus 10 No. 10	32

ALMIGHTY GOD SAID...
Opus 10 No. 1

Power, power
Power, power
Power, power
Power

The 1st Day

God said
"Let there be light
Call the light day
Call the darkness night
See that the light is good"

The 2nd Day

God said
"Let there be sky
Let there be water
Let there be dry ground
See that it is good"

The 3rd Day

God said
"Let there be days and years
And seasons
Let there also be stars
See that it is good"

The 4th Day

God said
"Let there be creatures in the sea
And let birds fly across the sky
See that it is good"

The 5th Day

God said
"Let there be creatures on the ground
Let there be animals
See that it is good"

The 6th Day

Then God said (x3)
"Let us create man in our image
See that it is all very good"

Very good (x3)

Creation

God created heaven and earth in six days

He is the Image of the Invisible God
Opus 10 No. 2

1st Chorus

Glorious, glorious, glorious
He
Glorious, glorious, glorious

2nd Chorus

He is glorious
All so beautiful
Yet all mine
Shining radiant
Glorious
He is the image
Glorious

1st Verse

He covers and rules all the regions
Whatever the thrones or dominions
He is the ultimate champion

2nd Verse

He sustains your very existence
Loving and caring with such kindness
Works in you and through you to bless

3rd Verse

The Father out of His good pleasure
Decided all fullness and treasure
To dwell within Him without measure

4th Verse

His blood brings reconciliation
Away from evil thoughts and actions
Presenting you as pure and holy

3rd Chorus

He is the image
So, take your courage
And touch Him
He is glorious

Shining radiant
All so beautiful
Yet all mine

Glorious
Glorious
He, He
He, He

Bridge

Radiant, radiant, radiant
Glorious
Radiant, radiant
He is radiant, He

He is radiant, He
Radiant
Glorious

4th Chorus

Glorious, glorious, glorious
He, He
He, He
Glorious, glorious, glorious
He, He
He, He

The Separating Veil is Torn!
Opus 10 No. 3

Chorus

Argh!

Torn! Torn! Torn! Torn!
Torn! Torn! Torn! Torn!

Interlude

Torn, torn, torn, torn
Torn, torn, torn, torn

1st Verse

In times B. C.
We could not see, see, see
The glory and the wonder of the LORD

2nd Verse

A curtain in place
We could not see His face, face, face
Only priests dare went to the LORD

3rd Verse

In fear we stayed
Our seeing kept; veiled

Could not go direct to the Father

4th Verse (repeat)

But now the veil is gone
Torn from top to bottom
Torn! Torn! Torn!
And Jesus bids us, us, us, us

"Enter"

5th Verse

In times B. C.
We could not see, see, see
The glory and the wonder of the LORD

6th Verse

A curtain in place
We could not see His face, face, face
Only priests dare went to the LORD

7th Verse

In fear we stayed
Our seeing kept; veiled
Could not go direct to the Father

8th Verse (repeat)

But now the veil is gone
Torn from top to bottom

16

Torn! Torn! Torn!
And Jesus bids us, us, us, us

Bridge

Torn from top to bottom
Torn

(Continuation)

And Jesus bids us

"Enter(!)"

Christ the Rising Star
Blink to the Moon!
Opus 10 No. 4

1st Verse

Blink, blink
Blink to the Moon
Jesus the Saviour
Is famous for ever
Blink, blink
Blink to the Moon
Jesus the Saviour
Is famous for ever
For ever and ever
For every believer

Blink! Blink! Blink!

2nd Verse

Blink, blink
Blink to the Moon
Resplendent and bright
The dazzling light
Blink, blink
Blink to the Moon
Resplendent and bright
The dazzling light
For ever and ever
For every believer

Blink! Blink! Blink! Blink! Blink!

3rd Verse

Blink, blink
Blink to the Moon
Encourage your cheer
His rising is here
Blink, blink
Blink to the Moon
Encourage your cheer
His rising is here
For ever and ever
For every believer

Blink! Blink! Blink!

Bridge

His rising
His rising
His rising
His rising

And higher
And higher
And higher
And higher!

The Star in the East!

B-link! Blink! Blink!
B-link! Blink! Blink!
B-link! Blink! Blink!
B-link! Blink! Blink!
B-link! Blink! Blink!
B-link! Blink! Blink!

Blink Blink Blink

His rising
His rising
His rising
His rising

And higher
And higher
And higher
And higher!

The Star in the East!

4th Verse

Blink, blink
Blink to the Moon
Jesus the Saviour
Is famous for ever
For ever and ever
For every believer
Resplendent and bright
The dazzling light
For ever and ever
For every believer
Encourage your cheer
His rising is here
For ever and ever
For every believer!

The Shulammite Woman
Opus 10 No. 5

"Shulammite
Shulammite"

1st & 3rd Verse

Oh, the shells of my heart
Longs for the songs to waft
And see her from the start
Stark songs so sweet and soft

2nd & 4th Verse

Sing sweetly my Shulammite
Sing melodies with your King
My treasured one sing tonight
Your King, too, a melody will bring

5th Verse

Here comes the chariot
From circling Sun and Moon
The Lion of Judah
Yearns the Shulammite tune

6th Verse

The King, too, sings melodies
The Shulammite so desires

None shall sing until ready
Duets burn like pure fire

7th Verse

Sing, sweetly my Shulammite
Your King yearns your offering
My treasured one, let us sing tonight
Let us never stop our dancing!

Chorus

Dance, dancing
Dance, dancing
Dance, dancing
Sing sweetly my Shulammite!

Sing
Sing
Sing
Sing sweetly my Shulammite!

Sing
Sing
Sing
Sing sweetly my Shulammite!

"Sing sweetly my King and my Shulammite"
My Shulammite
Sing
Sing sweetly my Shulammite!

Sing
Shulammite!

My Eternal Peace
Opus 10 No. 6

1st Chorus

God's peace

Do not be anxious
About anything
But in everything
Pray to Almighty

This peace from God guards me

Before my eyes open in the morning

1st Verse

Before my eyes open in the morning
At the instance of emerging from sleep
Even before I am aware of anything external
I experience something so powerful and so deep

2nd Verse

It is the start of a brand-new day
I rise and prepare for its future
Knowing this peace will not be fazed
Because it is an inexhaustible treasure

3rd Verse

Sometimes you can see it in my eyes
Or hear it behind my voice
It has something of eternal life in it
And inwardly I choose to rejoice

4th Verse

When the day turns into history
And I retire in the evening in peace
I rest sweetly on my cosy pillow
And before long I am fast asleep

5th Verse

This peace is from God and it guards me
Jesus left it here two thousand years ago
The first to have it were the Disciples
A special gift you can know

2nd Chorus

Do not be anxious
About anything
But in everything
Pray to Almighty

Ah
Ah
Ah
Ah

Before my eyes open in the morning

The Alternative Three Magi!
Opus 10 No. 7

Everyone

*"It was the first century...
and Herod had just lost the
seasonal supermarket chain war
– again...!"*

1st Verse

From all the way in Lapland
To Bethlehem with presents
Came Santa Claus and Rudolf
Wearing their bright green panties

Santa Claus gave lace up boots
Much bigger than stocking size
He also gave shaving kit
For when Jesus gets baptised

Mr Spock!

2nd Verse

Mr Spock from the Starship
Came from yonder Galaxy
His gift for the young baby
Was a large tube of Smarties

He also had other gifts
From great planets far and wide

But he lost them all
Oh dear!
When the Starship fell over

3rd Verse

The third wiseman was lanky
He wrote music for the Tsars
Moved from Russia to the States
This Sergei Rachmaninoff

His gift was not all that good
But must be played with left toe
Softly and quietly
A lullaby for a King
A full-size grand piano

Traditional Polish Lullaby

Close your eyes, Jesus, dear
Hush all Your sighing
Mary is holding You
No need for crying

Jauchzet Frohlocket - After J. S. Bach
Opus 10 No. 8

Strings
Strings and trumpets
And trumpets
And trumpets
Strings
Strings and trumpets
And trumpets
And trumpets
Strings
And trumpets
And trumpets
And trum!

Sing, you choir, loud and clear!
Let your voice be heard
Let it pierce the air
Pierce it once, pierce it twice
Angelic hosts
Angelic hosts
Angelic hosts
Pierce it thrice!

Move decisively
Move decisively
Move decisively
Left and right
Dance the dance
Day and night
From the slayer
Lightning flashes!
From his eye
From the slayer
Flash!

Move decisively
Move decisively
Move decisively
Left and right
Dance the dance
Day and night

From his eye
Lightning flashes!
A time of war
A time of clashes!

The command has come
Slay! Slay! Slay! Slay!
You cannot escape
On that dreaded Day

This high music is for you!
Cue higher music, cue
Let it ring
Clear and clarion!
It is for you and you
It is for you
It is your companion

Move, death angel
To and fro
Let all the people know
Yesterday, tomorrow, today
That you, Lord God
Have come to

Slay! Slay! Slay!

The Seven Spirits of Christ
Opus 10 No. 9

1ˢᵗ Chorus

Spirit calls
Hungry souls
Angels search

Heaven and Earth

Spirit calls
Hungry souls
Angels search

Heaven and Earth

Spirit calls
Hungry souls
Angels search

Heaven and Earth

Earth, Earth, Earth, Earth
Earth, Earth, Earth, Earth

Spirit calls
Hungry souls
Angels search

1ˢᵗ Verse

Throughout the World
Throughout the World

A trumpet sound
A trumpet sound
Is heard aloud
Is heard aloud
A trumpet sounds

2nd Verse

To Earth He comes
To Earth He comes
Our Lord a bounds
Our Lord a bounds
On greater clouds
On greater clouds
Our Lord a bounds

3rd Verse

Then judgement falls
Then judgement falls
As the Lion roars
As the Lion roars
His tongue projects
His tongue projects
Striking nations

4th Verse

Treading winepress
Treading winepress
Of God's anger
Of God's anger
His enemies
His enemies

Cannot escape
Throughout the World
Throughout the World
A trumpet sound
A trumpet sound
Is heard aloud
Is heard aloud
A trumpet sounds

KING AND LORD OF ALL

Solo

King and Lord of all
Our eternal light
For ever is Christ
Our eternal Christ

2nd Chorus

Spirit calls
Spirit calls
Hungry souls
Hungry souls
Angels search
Angels search

3rd Chorus

Spirit calls!

Heaven and Earth!
Heaven and Earth!
Heaven and Earth!
Heaven and Earth!

Calls!

Heaven and Earth!
Heaven and Earth!
Heaven and Earth!
Heaven and Earth!

Christ Jesus the Beau
Opus 10 No. 10

Chorus

Soprano, Alto:

See you later
See you later
Later you see
See you later
Revelation
The Prophet

1st Verse

Soprano, Alto:

So, He cocked His weapon did the Beau
And aimed it straight at the foe
Given it both barrels
Obliterating death in one go

Chorus

Soprano, Alto:

See you later
See you later
Later you see
See you later
Revelation

The Prophet

1ˢᵗ Verse – *variation*

Soprano, Alto:

So, He cocked His weapon did the Beau

Tenor:

You have had your all

Soprano, Alto:

And aimed it straight at the foe

Tenor:

And breathed your last breath

Soprano, Alto:

Giving it both barrels

Tenor:

Terminate you

Soprano, Alto:

Obliterating death in one go

Chorus

Soprano, Alto:

See you later
See you later
Later you see
See you later
Revelation
The Prophet

2nd Verse

Soprano, Alto:

No longer can it terrorise

Tenor:

Go and take a hike

Soprano, Alto:

Making people run in fear

Tenor:

Don't ever come back

Soprano, Alto:

Playing the fear game

Tenor:

Terminate you

Soprano, Alto:

Finality and end now the same

Chorus

Soprano, Alto:

See you later
See you later
Later you see
See you later
Revelation
The Prophet

3rd Verse

Soprano, Alto:

Yanked and thrown off the train of life

Tenor:

Don't ever call us

Soprano, Alto:

Mustering no resistance

Tenor:

And we won't call you

Soprano, Alto:

Destroyed for ever

Tenor:

Terminate you

Soprano, Alto:

No longer having an existence

Bass:

Revelation
Revelation

4th Verse – 'Heaven's Anthem'

Now, life and love and laughter
Embraces fullness and freedom and fraternity
And creativity and comfort and compassion
Lives in excitement and existence for eternity

4th Verse – 'Heaven's Anthem' *(triumphantly)*

Now, life and love and laughter
Embraces fullness and freedom and fraternity
And creativity and comfort and compassion
Lives in excitement and existence for eternity